MISS DOOFEY OPOSSUM

Anne Boykin

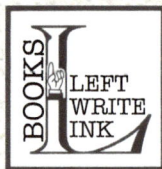

BOOKS LEFT WRITE INK

Copyright 2019 by Anne Boykin, Left-Write Ink, College Station, Texas

Text, book design, and illustrations by Anne Boykin
LWInk2@aol.com

Library of Congress Control Number: 2019902758
ISBN-13: 978-0-9761301-9-2

For

Tamara Anne

and

Thomas Arthur

December 25, 1986

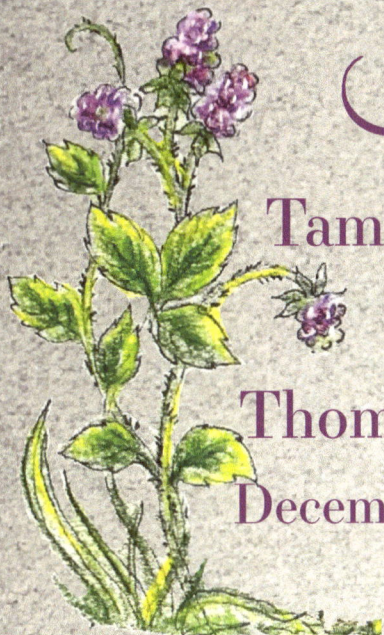

A
very
true story

'Twas a dark and stormy night.

A bit of moon was the only light.

Uncle Thomas and his best friend, Chet,

set out to rescue an opossum pet.

As they drove Old Highway Six,
they recalled past
back-road trips. . .
swimming the Brazos among
the snakes,
and looking for turtles at
Country Club Lake.

Many animals from far and wide,
knew Uncle Thomas and Chet
were on their side.

Suddenly, in the moonlight shone,
an orphaned opossum. . .all alone.

Uncle Thomas hit the brakes!

The baby opossum began to shake!

Soon, his gentle hands

engulfed her and

in his pocket, he gently placed her.

Once at home, they made a bed,

of an old shoe box,

and rags they had shred.

Wild infant formula they warmed

for her tummy,

of milk and egg yolks that

tasted so yummy.

Out of a dropper,

the formula she lapped.

And when she was full,

she napped. . .and she napped!

Every two hours, this schedule they kept.

And once in a while. . .
Uncle Thomas? He slept!

From Austin came Tamara and young Thomas Arthur.

They greeted the opossum with squeals and with laughter.

They fed her and pet her and
cuddled her and then. . .
rocked her. . .and loved her. . .and
started over again.

That Uncle Thomas was such an

old softy,

he gave them the baby whom they

promptly named. . .

DOOFY

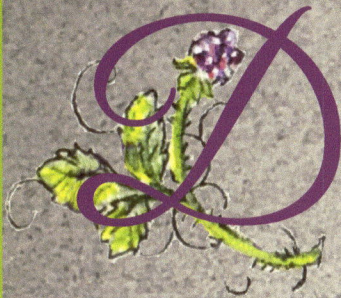

Doofey was nurtured with
love and she grew,
to be the sweetest opossum anyone
ever knew.

An opossom is a marsupial,
that is quite nocturnal.
The hours she kept were
quite infernal!

She slept all day and
played all night,
and hung by her tail,
in the bright moonlight.

Her beady, black eyes saw best
in the night,
and her soft, little ears tuned in
with delight.

She nibbled on puppy food
and loved scrambled eggs.

Milk, she would lap. . .

. . .right

. . .down

. . .to the

. . .dregs.

Baths were a favorite part
of Miss Doofey's routine.

Her tiny pink tongue licked her
hands quite clean and
rubbing them over her face it
would seem,

That no child had
. . .ever
. . .EVER been this clean!

And so, Miss Doofey spent
her life at ease,
eating, and sleeping,
and playing to please.

Tamara and Thomas Arthur gave
her love day by day,
which she gave back to them
in all sorts of ways.

Such is the story of
Miss Doofey Opossum,
an orphan whose life
was allowed to blossom.

The End

Miss Doofey and Tamara Anne
Bastrop State Park, Texas, 1985

Miss Doofey Opossum came to our Gunter family in July of 1983 after her mother died beside the road near College Station, Texas. My younger brother Thomas Boykin and his best friend, Chet Churchill, rescued this little orphan opossum. Of the eight babies in her mother's pouch, only one female survived. She was one month old and barely four inches long. We called her Doodley Squat at first and eventually she became known as Miss Doofey.

Thomas and Chet, from the time they were young boys playing along Bee Creek and the Brazos River, had long been known to the Texas A&M University Biology Department as extremely knowledgeable sources of information and specimens for their research. Many of the boys' snakes, turtles, tortoises, and opossums were documented, cared for, and later released back into the wild. They could rattle off the genus and species names of each and every critter known to Texas. Now, as grown men with families of their own, their studies and love of the wild animals of the Brazos Valley continues.

As for Miss Doofey, her short, but sweet, life was a constant source of entertainment and education for our family, as well as for the children of the neighborhood, the Scout troops, and the classrooms where she visited often. Because she was deprived of the nutrition her mother's milk would have provided, her bones did not develop as strong as they should have. She was unable to survive in the wild and needed the care of our loving family.

If you are thinking about trying to acquire a pet opossum for yourself...DON'T! Miss Doofey was a very special case. She was rescued and handled by knowledgeable wildlife specialists, as well as a licensed veterinarian. Miss Doofey passed away in her sleep at the age of 3-1/2 years, much longer than had she been left to fend for herself in the wild.

Contact your state Parks and Wildlife Department if you see an abandoned or injured wild animal. They have trained volunteers who are licensed to care for them and hopefully, get them back into the wild.

Miss Doofey in the bluebonnets, May 1984

For more information:
Texas Parks and Wildlife Department
https://tpwd.texas.gov/huntwild/wild/rehab/orphan

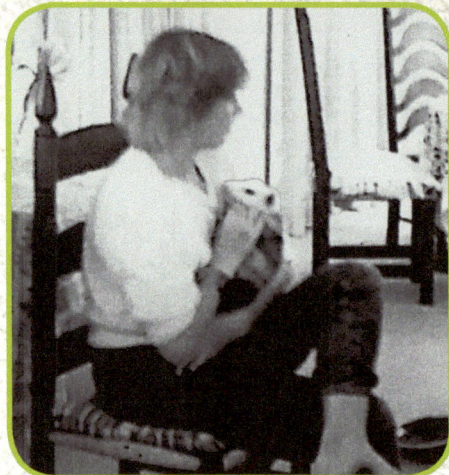

MISS DOOFEY
with Gunters & Petersons

Clockwise from left:
· *Miss Doofey in the loving arms of Tamara.*
· *Peterson cousins Lance, Daren, Ryan with*
  Thomas, Tamara, and Miss Doofey
· *Just swinging at the park*
· *Tamara, Thomas Arthur, and Miss Doofey*
  with the Peterson cousins at their fishing
  cabin, Inter Coastal Canal, Gulf of Mexico

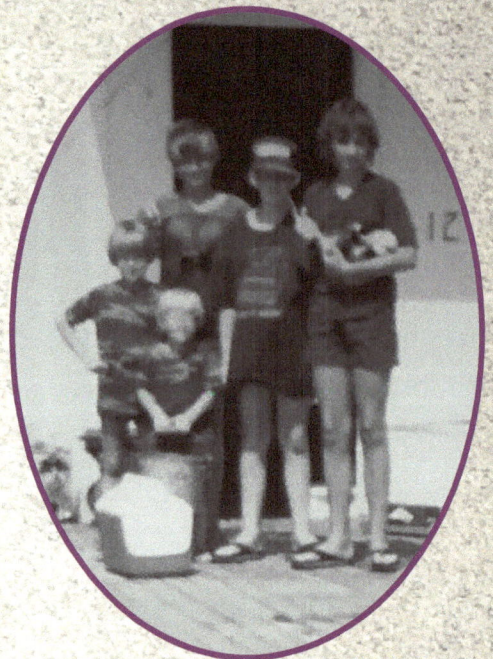

Counter clockwise from right: ·
· Miss Doofey plays in her tree
· Cousin Ryan and Miss Doofey
· Miss Doofey as a baby
· Tamara and Miss Doofey

Chet
Churchill

Thomas
Boykin

THOMAS
& CHET

Lifetime Best Friends

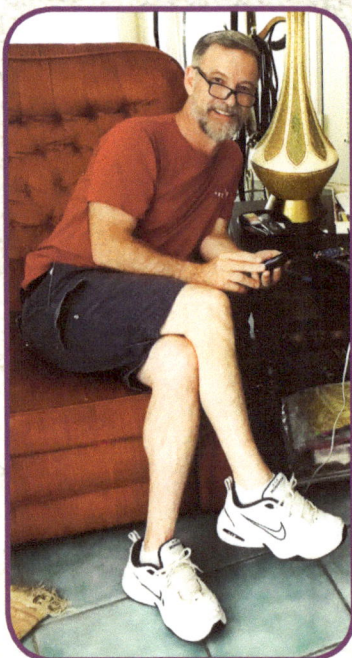

Chet Churchill, 2018

Thomas Boykin, 2018

Chet and Speckled
King Snake, June 1970

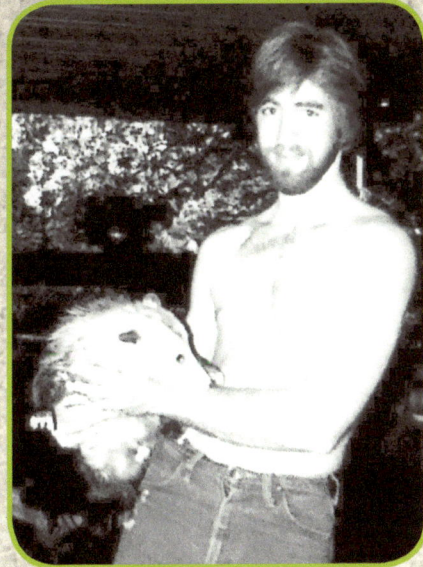
Thomas and
Miss Doofey, 1985

Thomas and PJ 'Possum, 1973

Chet and Mexican
Milk Snake, 1994

VIRGINIA OPOSSUM
(Didelphis virginiana)

Description

Opossums are cat-sized mammals with a pointed snout, grayish fur, small ears, and a long, scaly tail. It can use its tail to hang from tree branches, and it has paws with opposable "thumbs." Males are usually larger and heavier than females.

Life History

The opossum is active only at night, and is a solitary animal. They have an eclectic diet and will eat both plants and animals, including rodents, young rabbits, birds, insects, crustaceans, frogs, fruits, berries, and vegetables.

Females usually have two litters a year. The babies are born after just 11-12 days, and are about the size of a honeybee. They are blind, furless, and do not look anything like adult opossums. After they are born, they crawl all by themselves unaided into their mother's pouch and immediately begin to nurse. Soon after the baby begins to nurse, the nipple swells and completely fills the baby opossum's mouth, causing it to be firmly attached to its mother. It remains attached until it is about 7 weeks old, at which time it has grown large enough to detach itself. This unusual adaptation helps make up for the short gestation period. Many opossums die during the first year of their life, and adults usually live only about two years in the wild.

Habitat

Opossums are primarily woodland creatures, but are also frequently found in prairies, marshes, and farmlands. Although they prefer to live in hollow trees and logs, opossums will also shelter in woodpiles, rock piles, crevices in cliffs, under buildings, in attics, and in abandoned underground burrows dug by other animals.

Distribution

Opossums occur statewide except for the arid Trans-Pecos and Llano Estacado of the Panhandle.

Other

Opossums, as a group, are among the oldest, most primitive mammals of the New World. Some scientists call them "living fossils" because they have survived relatively unchanged for at least 50 million years. They are intermediate in many respects between the most primitive of all mammals, the egg-laying monotremes of Australia, and the higher placental mammals. Their chief character is the marsupium or pouch that develops on the abdomen of females. They have 50 teeth which is more than any other mammal. Humans normally have 32 teeth. A recent study found that one opossum can consume around 5,000 ticks a year. They are rabies resistant. Only one species of opossum occurs in Texas.

Sources: Texas Parks and Wildlife Department and Cary Institute

Source: Wikimedia Commons

About the Author/Illustrator

An accomplished artist, illustrator, and calligrapher who spent 30 years in Austin, Texas, Anne Boykin returned to her home town of College Station, Texas, in 2004. She quickly made her mark in the community working for the City of College Station managing Project HOLD -- an historic online library database dedicated to historic preservation efforts. (HOLD.cstx.gov)

In 2011, Anne joined the Texas A&M University Engineering Extension Service (TEEX) as a graphic designer. Her book designs, created for TEEX, won four national awards. Anne also designed a 45' installation chronicling the history of the Brayton Fire Field in College Station. Another 30' installation in Fort Worth chronicles TEEX and OSHA history.

Recent freelance work involved creating historical military maps for authors that appear in five books. Her expertise is evident in noted public installations of 23 historical interpretive panels for the Lynn Stuart Pathway at Veterans Park & Athletic Complex in College Station and 15 historical interpretive panels for Boonville Heritage Park in neighboring Bryan, Texas.

The author and her brother
Thomas Heath Boykin
March 2018

With retirement in 2017 came the opportunity for Anne to work on her own book projects. *The Christmas Chameleon, A Colorful Tale*, was published in December 2017. The second edition, *The Christmas Chameleon, A Colorful Tail & Coloring Book*, was published in 2018. Next on her list is *To Get to Here, A Journey through My Childhood, 1953 - 1963* due to be published in the summer of 2019.

Anne attended both Texas A&M University and Arizona State University. She has two children, three grandchildren, and two grand dogs, all of whom she adores.

Thomas Arthur and Tamara Anne Gunter
May 1976

GrAnne and her G-kids: Forrest,
Thomas Allen, and Ava Gunter
December 2017

Thomas Arthur and
Tamara Anne, 2019

The Original "Miss Doofey"

In 1985, I enrolled in a six week calligraphy workshop studying traditional manuscript book design. Miss Doofey had recently passed away. My children were saddened at the loss of such a special and beloved pet. Miss Doofey's story became my project for the class.

Composing the epic poem was first on the list. That certainly took a while. Poetry had always been an interest for me but this was the first time I had tackled an epic poem. Armed with a rhyming dictionary and lots of fond memories of Miss Doofey and her miracle story, I, literally, put pen to paper.

In choosing the materials with which to work, I first selected the gray Canson Mi Tientes paper because it reminded me of Miss Doofey's soft gray and white fur. It also had a bit of "tooth" that would hold up well to the calligraphy nib. Traditional book design allows for large margins so that fingerprints and smudges would not destroy the calligraphy or the artwork. The design also utilizes the Golden Mean, the same mathematical proportions used in creating the Pyramids of Giza, the Greek temples, the Mona Lisa, and even our own bodies.

Using a purple watercolor gouache to make the ink, I applied the gouache to the Brause steel nib with a brush and began to calligraph. There were many rewrites in my efforts to make it perfect. Fortunately, I had bought 25 sheets of the Canson paper.

Once the text was complete, the illustrations were next. Using Faber Castell Design Spectracolor pencils and Japanese stick ink, I drew and inked in the illustrations several times before drawing them directly on the pages. It was difficult trying to capture the softness of Miss Doofey's fur and her sweet expression. But I persevered.

I bound and covered the book boards with a soft gray Japanese paper with pale white speckles. A pink grosgrain ribbon, reminiscent of Miss Doofey's rough tongue and tail, was added as a bookmark. Sadly, the bookmark disappeared some years ago.

the formula she lapped, and
when she was full, she napped...
and she napped!

Twenty years later, somewhere around 2005, the epic poem of Miss Doofey's life won a poetry contest in Brazos Valley. I recall being asked to do a few readings at the Hastings book store one Saturday afternoon. Fame was fleeting and Miss Doofey's book was put on the shelf until I began dragging it out to read to my nieces, nephews, and years later, my grandchildren.

The Miss Doofey book has always been on my list of "things to do" when I retire. Now, was the time. But first, the book needed to be reformatted to make it suitable for young readers. Sadly, few children can read the italic script calligraphy. Essones was chosen as a readable font. And more illustrations were added to better capture the interest of children. My hope is that this book will pique the interest of the reader to have an appreciation for North America's only native marsupial.

Anne Boykin

Acknowledgments

This world would be a better place if more children had the opportunity to develop an appreciation for life as experienced in nature observing and interacting with the wildlife that surrounds us. Had it not been for my brother **Thomas Boykin** and his best friend **Chet Churchill** and their absolute love of nature, this story would not have happened. Their assistance in helping me create this book was vital. Their self-motivated quest for knowledge is incredible and inspiring. I love you guys!

My daughter **Tamara Gunter** has been my creative inspiration ever since she began to dabble in art as a young girl. In later years, it was obvious that she had a true gift for design, not only in art but in everything she touched. I have always sought and valued her opinion, eagle eye, and approval in my projects. Her blessing of this book was critical to me. Showing her continued love of the animal world, she has fostered 40 or more Golden Retrievers through the years. Thank you, sweetie!

My son **Thomas Arthur Gunter**, grew up playing in Bull Creek in Austin, Texas. Watching him, as a young boy, drag home critters reminded me of watching my little brother. Thomas Arthur has raised his children in Scouting programs, family camping trips, and being a wonderful hands on parent. They are becoming fine young adults. I am most proud of this family. Thomas and my grandchildren are part of my inspiration for publishing this book. Thank you, sweetie!

My dear grade school friend for 64 years (so far), **Allan Riggs**, has shown incredible patience and offered constant support as I toiled over this book. Allan's upbeat personality, quick wit, and sense of humor sustained me whenever I hit a stumbling block. Thank you!

www.ingramcontent.com/pod-product-compliance
Lightning Source LLC
Chambersburg PA
CBHW061100090426
42742CB00003B/102